Most dinosaurs had tough, scaly skin.

Long, strong tail

Many dinosaurs were very big. Allosaurus was 40 ft (12.2 m) long and 17 ft (5.2 m) tall.

Allosaurus

Clawed foot

Stand up!

Unlike today's lizards, dinosaurs had legs that tucked under their body. A lizard's legs jut out at an angle.

5

The dinosaur age

Dinosaurs roamed the Earth for 165 million years. The world was warmer then, with no ice caps. Many different species lived through this long span of time. The age of the dinosaurs is divided into the Triassic, Jurassic, and Cretaceous periods.

The Jurassic period started about 200 mya and lasted for 55 million years.

Dinosaurs appeared during the Triassic period, about 230 mya.

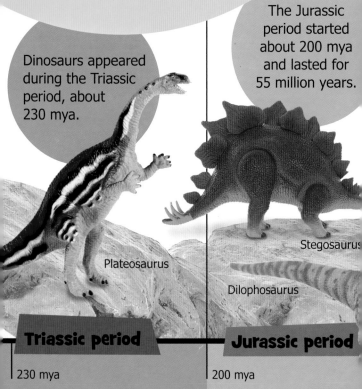

Plateosaurus

Stegosaurus

Dilophosaurus

Triassic period

230 mya

Jurassic period

200 mya

DINOS

Contents

What is a dinosaur?

Giant dinosaurs were the biggest animals ever to live on land. There were hundreds of different dinosaurs, and they roamed the earth for 165 million years. They looked like "terrible lizards," which is what the word "dinosaur" means.

Meat-eating dinosaurs had sharp teeth and powerful jaws. But many dinosaurs ate only plants.

Dinosaurs had small brains and were not very intelligent.

Giant eggs

Fossilized dinosaur eggs

Dinosaurs were reptiles. Like the reptiles alive today, dinosaurs hatched from eggs.

The dinosaur information box tells you:

- how to say the dinosaur's name
- what the dinosaur's hips were like
- when the dinosaur lived
- how big the dinosaur was

Mya

We have abbreviated **million years ago** to **mya.**

The Cretaceous period started 145 mya and lasted for 80 million years.

T. rex

Gallimimus

Cretaceous period

145 mya

We are much closer in time to T. rex than T. rex was to Plateosaurus.

7

Dinosaur hips

Dinosaurs were only named 200 years ago. At first, it was very hard to figure out how to fit the giant bones that people had found together. But as more complete dinosaur skeletons were discovered, people divided them into two groups, depending on whether their hips were arranged like the hips of a bird or those of a lizard.

Hip bones

Allosaurus skeleton

Lizard-hipped

Allosaurus was in the lizard-hipped group. Some lizard-hipped dinosaurs walked on two legs and ate meat, like Allosaurus. Others, like Diplodocus walked on four legs and ate plants.

- Al-uh-SAWR-us
- lizard-hipped
- late Jurassic period
- 40 ft (12.2 m) long, 17 ft (5.2 m) tall

Stegosaurus was in the bird-hipped group. All bird-hipped dinosaurs were plant-eaters.

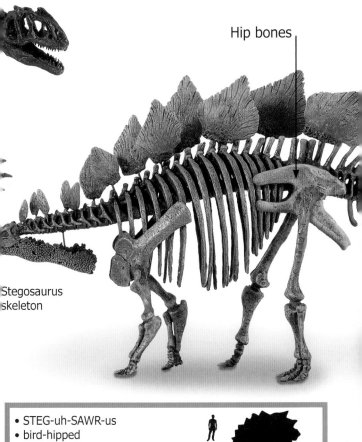

Hip bones

Stegosaurus skeleton

- STEG-uh-SAWR-us
- bird-hipped
- late Jurassic period
- 28 ft (8.5 m) long, 14 ft (4.3 m) tall

Iguanodon

Iguanodon fossils have been found in Europe, Africa, and North America. It was one of the first dinosaurs to be named, in 1825. Iguanodon had a sharp, horny beak for breaking off plants and strong cheek teeth for grinding up food.

Plants wore down Iguanodon's horny beak, but it kept on growing.

Iguanodon had big, fleshy cheeks and could keep food in its mouth while it chewed.

Rip and grasp

Iguanodon had a sharp thumb claw for ripping off leaves. A bendable finger helped it to grasp plants tightly.

Thumb

Ig-WAN-oh-don
bird-hipped
early Cretaceous period
26 ft (7.9 m) long,
6 ft (4.9 m) tall

Iguanodon
had a long,
stiff tail.

Grind it up!

Iguanodon's rows
of teeth moved both
up and down and from
side to side to grind
tough leaves
and twigs.

Iguanodon walked
on its toes. It
had small hooves
instead of claws.

Iguanodon's front legs could reach the ground,
but its back legs were longer and stronger.

11

Ankylosaurus

Built like a tank, Ankylosaurus was very good at defending itself. Its body was covered in tough, bony plates, and one swing of its heavy tail club was enough to break an attacker's leg!

Ankylosaurus moved slowly, eating plants close to the ground.

Even its eyelids were armor-plated!

The solid, bone club was a very dangerous weapon!

- Ang-KILE-uh-SAWR-us
- bird-hipped
- late Cretaceous period
- 35 ft (10.6 m) long, 11 ft (3.4 m) tall

Strong muscles made it possible for Ankylosaurus to swing its heavy tail club from side to side.

Its soft belly was the only part of Ankylosaurus' body that was not covered in bony plates!

Gas factory!

Ankylosaurus did not have lots of teeth for chewing up plants. It probably just waited for the food to break down in its stomach. This would have produced large amounts of gas!

Small teeth

Parasaurolophus

A peaceful dinosaur, Parasaurolophus lived in family groups, or herds, grazing on plants. It could see and hear well and had a good sense of smell. This helped it to be alert to possible dangers.

- Par-ah-SAWR-OL-uh-fus
- bird-hipped
- late Cretaceous period
- 33 ft (10.1 m) long, 16 ft (4.9 m) tall

Crests

The duck-billed dinosaurs all had hollow crests in different shapes.

Corythosaurus

Lambeosaurus

14

Parasaurolophus had a hollow, bony crest. It probably used this a bit like a trumpet, making loud, honking noises to warn the herd of danger.

Parasaurolophus was a duck-billed dinosaur. Its bony beak was good for plucking leaves to eat.

When it was eating, Parasaurolophus walked on four legs. But to get away, it ran on two legs.

Tough teeth

Behind its bony beak, Parasaurolophus had hundreds of teeth for grinding up the tough plants it ate.

Rows of teeth

Saurolophus

Triceratops

Triceratops had a large, bony head frill and three sharp horns. It lived peacefully in herds, grazing on plants, but would charge to frighten away an attacking dinosaur.

Charge!

Triceratops could charge at up to 25 mph (40 kph).

- Try-SAIR-uh-tops
- bird-hipped
- late Cretaceous period
- 26 ft (7.9 m) long, 9.5 ft (2.9 m) tall

Its bony head frill protected Triceratops from attack.

Triceratops weighed more than 11,000 lb (5000 kg), as much as an elephant.

Giant skull

Triceratops' massive skull could be over 10 ft (3 m) long, one-third the length of its body.

Triceratops used its beak to pick plants.

Hundreds of teeth in its jaws sliced up the leaves.

Pachycephalosaurus

Pachycephalosaurus was a "thick-headed lizard" with a large dome of bone on its head. It was a plant-eating, bird-hipped dinosaur. It may have used the thick skull to fight other males, just like mountain sheep today.

Pachycephalosaurus had short arms that ended in clawed hands with five fingers.

- Pak-ee-SEF-uh-lo-SAWR-us
- bird-hipped
- late Cretaceous period
- 18 ft (5.5 m) long, 10 ft (3.1 m) tall

Other boneheads

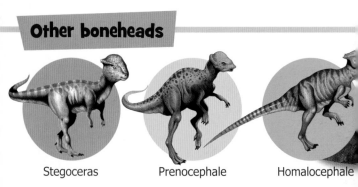

Stegoceras   Prenocephale   Homalocephale

18

The bone on Pachycephalosaurus' skull could be 10 in (25 cm) thick.

Bony knobs stuck out of the side and back of its skull.

Tiny teeth

Pachycephalosaurus had small, sharp teeth. It ate fruit, seeds, and soft plants.

Long, heavy tail

Pachycephalosaurus had claws on its feet, but only three toes.

Diplodocus

With its long neck and tail, Diplodocus was one of the longest-ever land animals. It was a peaceful creature that grew to a huge size by eating plants alone.

Diplodocus' neck could be as long as 26 ft (8 m).

Diplodocus had a tiny head and brain.

The longer its neck, the more a dinosaur could eat from one spot without moving its body.

Diplodocus' flat, padded feet were so large that you could have had a bath in one of the footprints!

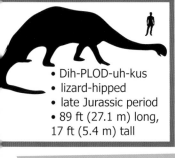

- Dih-PLOD-uh-kus
- lizard-hipped
- late Jurassic period
- 89 ft (27.1 m) long, 17 ft (5.4 m) tall

Other big vegetarians

Apatosaurus

Camarasaurus

Brachiosaurus

Dinosaur bones are hollow, like those of a bird. This is part of the reason why it was possible for dinosaurs to become so large.

Diplodocus had extra bones under its backbone to give its long neck and tail additional support.

Strong legs

Feeble teeth

Vegetarian dinosaurs often had weak teeth and could not chew plants. So they swallowed stones, which helped to grind up the food in their stomach.

Mamenchisaurus

21

T. rex

Tyrannosaurus rex was one of the largest meat-eaters ever to walk on the planet. Fierce and fearless, it hunted alone. Its name means "king of the tyrant reptiles."

As a hunter, T. rex needed very good eyesight.

T. rex used its long, heavy tail to balance its big head.

Skull and teeth

T. rex had a huge skull, with jaws so big that it could have swallowed a human whole. Its teeth grew as long as 17 in (18 cm), with an edge as sharp and serrated as a kitchen knife.

- Tye-RAN-uh-SAWR-us rex
- lizard-hipped
- late Cretaceous period
- 50 ft (15.2 m) long, 23 ft (7 m) tall

Its massive skull was so strong that T. rex could cope with crashing into prey at 20 mph (32 kph).

T. rex's short arms were not long enough to reach its mouth.

Strong, powerful legs

Sharp claws

Spinosaurus

Ceratosaurus

Tarbosaurus

Allosaurus

23

Deinonychus

Deinonychus was small but it could outsprint much larger dinosaurs. It lived and hunted in packs, working together to attack and kill dinosaurs four or five times its size.

Deinonychus tore at its food with more than 60 knifelike teeth. They curved backwards to give a powerful bite.

Deinonychus had a big skull with a large brain. Hunting together required intelligence to time movements and coordinate the attack.

Deinonychus claw

Deinonychus was named for its terrible claws. When leaping to the attack, it could use the extra-large claw on each foot to cut a deep wound.

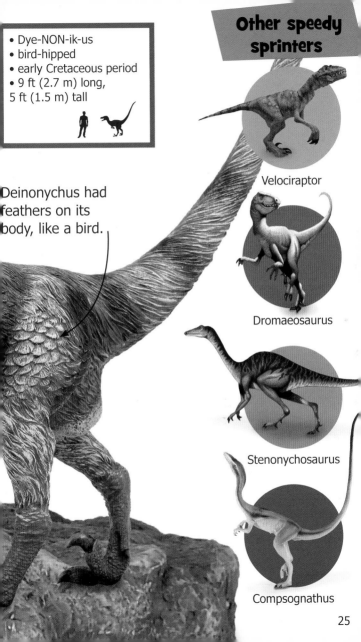

- Dye-NON-ik-us
- bird-hipped
- early Cretaceous period
- 9 ft (2.7 m) long,
  5 ft (1.5 m) tall

Deinonychus had feathers on its body, like a bird.

Other speedy sprinters

Velociraptor

Dromaeosaurus

Stenonychosaurus

Compsognathus

25

Spinosaurus

With its long tail and spiny sail, Spinosaurus was both longer and taller than T. rex. It was known as the "spiny lizard" because of the long spines on its back.

Long stiff tail

Spinosaurus had a sail along its back supported by long bones. ⎯⎯⎯⎯→

It had a long mouth and stabbing, cone-shaped teeth like those of a crocodile. It ate fish and other dinosaurs.

Clawed feet ⎯⎯→

26

Having the Sun shine on its tall, spiny sail may have helped Spinosaurus to warm up. If it was too hot, it could turn so that its sail did not face the Sun.

Clawed hand with three fingers

Powerful legs

- SPY-nuh-SAWR-us
- lizard-hipped
- Cretaceous period
- 40 ft (12.2 m) long, 14 ft (4.3 m) tall

The death of the dinosaurs

We have found out what we know about dinosaurs from the large bones and other fossils that have been discovered. These tell us that the last dinosaurs died out about 65 mya.

Scientists think that a huge asteroid crashed into the Earth at the end of the Cretaceous period.

Fossil life

Fossils are the remains of things that lived in earlier times. The most common fossils are made up of hard parts of the animal, such as the bones or shell.

With little warmth from the Sun, the temperature on Earth dropped to 14°F (-10°C).

Rock and dust blocked out the Sun's light.

Explosion!

It may be that it was not an asteroid, but a huge volcanic eruption that killed the dinosaurs. This would have blocked the Sun's light and cooled the Earth in the same way.

Glossary

This glossary explains some of the harder words in the book.

asteroid An object of rock or metal that travels around the Sun like a planet.

backbone The bony structure that runs along and supports an animal's back. Lots of bones link together to form the backbone.

beak A bony section sticking out at the front of the mouth. Dinosaurs used their beak to pluck food to eat.

bird-hipped Dinosaurs whose hip bones were shaped like those of a bird today. All bird-hipped dinosaurs ate only plants.

claw A sharp pointed nail growing at the end of a finger or toe.

crest The top part of the head. Some dinosaurs had a large crest for display or for making lots of noise.

Cretaceous The final period of time when dinosaurs lived on Earth, from 145 mya to 65 mya.

dinosaur A reptile that lived on land. Its legs tucked under its body.

fossil The remains of a living creature changed into a form that does not rot away.

ice caps Large areas of ice around the North and South Poles.

jaw The structure of bone that supports the mouth. Teeth are set into the jaw.

Jurassic The middle period of time when dinosaurs lived on Earth, from 200 mya to 145 mya.

lizard-hipped Dinosaurs whose hip bones were shaped like those of a lizard today. Some lizard-hipped dinosaurs ate meat, while others ate only plants.

meat-eating A dinosaur that attacked and ate animals and other dinosaurs.

pack A large group animals that lives ar hunts together.

plant-eating A dinosaur that ate only plants.

plates Hard sectio of skin that protecte the dinosaur from attack.

reptile A cold-blooded anim that lays eggs. Its s is scaly.

skeleton The hard structure that suppo an animal's body. A dinosaur's skeleton was made of bones.

skull The section of the skeleton that protects an animal's head. A number of bones join together form the skull.

Triassic The first period of time when dinosaurs lived on Earth, from 230 mya to 200 mya.

volcanic eruption When a volcano erupts, molten rock hurled out of a hole the ground known a the crater.